How to Understand Women Through Their Cats

How to Understand Women Through Their Cats

Wendy Diamond

Sterling Publishing Co., Inc.
NEW YORK

DEDICATION

*To all those lucky people who find love
through woman's best friend.*

Library of Congress Cataloging-in-Publication Data Available

2 4 6 8 10 9 7 5 3 1

Published by Sterling Publishing Co., Inc.
387 Park Avenue South, New York, NY 10016
© 2006 by Wendy Diamond
Distributed in Canada by Sterling Publishing
c/o Canadian Manda Group, 165 Dufferin Street
Toronto, Ontario, Canada M6K 3H6
Distributed in the United Kingdom by GMC Distribution Services
Castle Place, 166 High Street, Lewes, East Sussex, England BN7 1XU
Distributed in Australia by Capricorn Link (Australia) Pty. Ltd.
P.O. Box 704, Windsor, NSW 2756, Australia

Printed in China

Sterling ISBN-13: 978-1-4027-3095-5
ISBN-10: 1-4027-3095-0

For information about custom editions, special sales, premium and
corporate purchases, please contact Sterling Special Sales
Department at 800-805-5489 or specialsales@sterlingpub.com.

CONTENTS

INTRODUCTION

"I simply can't resist a cat, particularly the purring one. They are the cleanliest, cunningest, and most intelligent things I know, outside of the girl you love, of course."

HENRY W. FISHER, ABROAD WITH MARK TWAIN AND EUGENE FIELD

I had so many requests and inquiries from men after they read my last book, *How to Understand Men Through Their Dogs*, to find out more about women and their pets, I decided to write this book, *How to Understand Women Through Their Cats*. If dog is man's best friend, then it's safe to say that cat is woman's best friend. There are still eighty-five million singles in the United States looking for the perfect match, and through this book I hope to help men better understand their feline counterparts. The feminine mystique has been closely tied to the cat's characteristics—mysterious, independent, graceful, changeable, aloof, curious, finicky, and so on—for centuries.

A man can learn more about the woman in his life he wants to impress, date, or marry by the cat she owns and their shared personality traits. He will discover what makes the woman he adores purr, why his catlike companion takes her claws out when she does, whether his queen is really a feline fatale, and ultimately who is this unexplainable and timeless female creature that has captured men's hearts since the beginning of time!

In Chapter One, I provide you with a lesson in cat history and provide accurate accounts of how women and cats have shared some challenging and golden olden times. There are more than eighty-five million cats in the United States, and guaranteed that women share their lives with a lot of them. Since women naturally identify with cats, I explore the personality traits of the top twenty breeds of cat in the United States. Through research, my professional work experiences as founder and editorial director of *Animal Fair* magazine, and personally knowing many women with cats, in Chapter Two, I humorously compare the shared characteristics of each cat breed with its female owners. I provide men with the missing formula they all have been endlessly searching for: Will the Siamese Woman keep you up all night chatting? Who's the real hunter in your relationship—you or Ms. Main Coon? Is Ms. Manx a leader in her relationships, or does she always tail behind? I take my findings one step farther in Chapter Three and delightfully describe different types of women by the color of the cats they choose. Will a man be lucky or unlucky with a black or white cat? Which color of a cat needs more time at the gym? Does a tabby or tortie behave more naughtily?

When a man and a woman live together, it's an artful compromise and special dance that the two create together. In Chapter Four, I give men comical special tips on how to comfortably cohabitate with a woman and her cat(s), incorporating their unique habits, likes, and pet peeves. What do you do if your girlfriend or wife's cat insists on sleeping in your bed and then keeps you up all night? When is the most opportune time to give your woman—and cat—nip? And that age-old question: Who is really responsible for cleaning the litter box? In Chapter Five, I take living with a woman and her cat(s) one step farther. Men will find out what they can expect from different types of Cat Ladies by the number of cats they own. Is Cat Lady Two (lives with two cats) more practical in all areas of her life because of her feline strategies? Will Cat Lady Six (lives with six cats) stop at six cats, or will your life resemble that of a zookeeper? Is Cat Lady One (lives with one cat) truly satisfied with just one-to-one relationships?

I'm still single and dating and confide in my rescued Russian blue cat, Pasha, on matters of the heart. Yes, I'm a Cat Lady One, but with a catch: I also have a rescued Maltese dog named

Lucky. My cat and dog have created a special and unique bond together and enrich my life daily. Let this entertaining dating guidebook help you figure out more about the woman in your life by the cat(s) she shares her life with. And when you find the purrrfect feline for you, no thanks are necessary!

CHAPTER ONE

A Brief History of Cats and Women

*".... sometimes from her eyes I did receive
fair speechless messages."*

WILLIAM SHAKESPEARE, THE MERCHANT OF VENICE

Throughout time, cats have been thought of as mysterious, aloof, independent, and changeable, and they've been associated with women, who share the same qualities and personality traits. Both have survived and endured many different cycles of history to emerge stronger and more respected with the passing of time. Cats are mammals, descended from carnivores more than forty-five million years ago. They evolved depending on their hunting prowess, prey, and environment. Some modern-day women emulate the cat and might agree that their hunting skills regarding men and male habitat are a large motivator when choosing a place to live, socialize, or work.

Cats started the process of domestication themselves, for where there were men and women there was food, and where there was food there were mice and rats. Three different varieties of cats existed more than three million years ago: Panthera—big cats such as lions; Felis—smaller cats; and Acinonyx—the cheetah, which is the only cat whose claws fully retract. The first recorded cat to live with man was the African Wild Cat, which still exists today. Forty different species of cat presently roam the earth, except in Antarctica, where there are none.

Women can thank, and men can learn from, the ancient Egyptian civilization that adored and worshipped cats. Felines first protected and guarded the Egyptians' grain, their largest export, by chasing and hunting all the vermin away. Eventually, as each generation matured, cats began living in the Egyptians' homes, and regal domestication and sacred religious status ensued. Killing or hurting a cat was punishable by death. Men, you should always treat a woman and her cat(s) as the royalty that they truly are.

The Egyptians were very protective of their cats and wouldn't sell them. The Greeks, however, stole, bred, and sold cats to the Romans, Gauls, and Celts. They were bought primarily for mouse hunting and spread throughout civilizations.

One of the darkest periods in history for both cats and women came in the beginning of the sixteenth century, during the Inquisition. The crusaders and their loyalists killed and burned almost all the cats throughout Europe, as they were considered symbols of—and the incarnation of—the devil.

Single women with cats were suspect and considered witches. Perhaps this is why men in love feel bewitched by women. The senseless mutual persecution of both cats and women forever linked the two as kindred spirits.

Luckily, cats have nine lives, and one of their resurrections happened during the early eighteenth century, when plagues were brought to Europe by brown rats traveling on Chinese boats. The plagues threatened to kill millions of people, and cats were bred again to hunt the rats carrying the disease. People finally realized that cats weren't evil and allowed them to live and multiply freely.

The cat has been the inspirational muse for all types of artists, cartoonists, musicians, writers, poets, and the like for centuries. Recorded images of cats on paintings on tomb walls, in carved and sculpted statues, and as mummified remains are found as far back as forty-five hundred years ago. Some famous cat cartoon characters are Felix, Fritz, Garfield, and Heathcliff; the very first cartoon cat was Krazy Kat, who debuted back in 1913. Mark Twain loved cats and frequently wrote about his favorite animal. Then there are the more commercial cats, such as Leo the Lion—the famous MGM lion. And who can forget Morris, the 9Lives cat? The Broadway musical *Cats* had one of the longest recorded runs. The movies *Catwoman* and *Cat People* both brought to the silver screen the idea that female humans could be transformed into cat creatures. Males, beware! These are just a few examples in which cats have been immortalized through the arts.

Here is some fun folklore associated with cats! Mohammad's beloved cat was named Muzza, and it is believed that one night in the desert Mohammad ripped off one of his sleeves for his cat to sleep on, creating a special place for cats in Islam. Buddhists believed that upon death, the soul of a person that reached the highest level of spirituality would enter a cat; once the cat died, the soul went to paradise. Some weather forecasters claim that when rain threatens, a cat will stop playing, become still and thoughtful, or wash an ear. The most enduring cat myth—that a black cat brings bad luck—started in ancient China. Some English believe that if a woman of marriageable age nurses a cat on one knee she will remain single, and that young women fond of cats will live longer. See, men, you'll have a lifetime of happiness if you hook up with a woman with a feline!

CHAPTER TWO

Cat Breeds

"There are no ordinary cats."
COLETTE

When a woman is attracted to a certain breed of cat, there must be some type of natural identification; otherwise, she'd pick a dog or a bird instead. This playful chapter actually compares the traits of twenty top cat breeds with the temperament of the female human owner. Are certain breeds talkers, and will they keep you up all night? Which women are tricksters, ready to pounce on you when you least expect it? Which feline breed is most maternal, ready to provide a loving home, complete with a litter of kitties? Men, this personality breed guide will help you better understand the women in your life, and if you're thinking about buying or rescuing a cat for your favorite gal, find the breed that suits her best!

Abyssinian

Personality

Dear Aby! Fellas, right from the start, don't let this soft-spoken charmer fool you! Ms. Abyssinian is a ball of fire with a princess presence. When dating her, make sure you take her to as many festive activities as possible with your male friends. She prefers hanging out with the guys over spending time with other felines, as she finds them to be a bit too catty for her refined taste. If you're trying to win Ms. Abyssinian, treat her to a weekly membership at her favorite spa. She feels her absolute best when fit and groomed. Lucky you—when the spa leads to the altar! You'll find this high-energy woman to be a devoted wife and a fiercely defensive mother.

Finicky Feline

The Abyssinian woman will get upset and sullen if your profession takes you on the road frequently. She cringes at the thought of being left alone for long periods of time and craves constant companionship.

Cat's Meow

Fun, fun, fun! Ms. Abyssinian is the sporty type and will partake in playing all kinds of games with you—as long as you treat her as your equal.

American Shorthair

Personality

The ancestors of the American Shorthair Woman were the first to settle in North America from Europe. Ms. American Shorthair is a modern feline who can adapt quickly to the city or countryside. She's a tough cookie with a pioneering spirit and will choose a working career over being a stay-at-home mom. Men, it's not that she doesn't want children—she does! The American Shorthair Woman would prefer to bring home the mice and pay for a nanny while she's out leaving her scent on the world. It's really not such a bad deal, since this scenario will take some of the financial pressure off of you! Two heads and two paychecks are better than one!

Finicky Feline

The American Shorthair Woman wants to be praised for her successful career triumphs. She won't take kindly if her contributions to your shared lifestyle are taken for granted. Men—you've been forewarned.

Cat's Meow

Ms. American Shorthair is a busy career woman, but she's also a loving and devoted mother who takes great pride in having it all!

Angora

Personality

The angelic Angora Woman is looking for her very own Fred Astaire, suave tango dancer, or Mr. Right who can perform a pas de deux with her throughout a lifetime. She's a one-man woman. Ms. Angora prances on any stage with great grace and flow, as if she's walking on air. This woman loves to move, and a night on the town at a happening dance club where she can show off is a must date. Don't worry, men, you don't have to impress the Angora Woman on the dance floor or rush off to ballroom-dancing classes. She'll appreciate the fact that you're brave and will think you're one cool cat for trying. This well-mannered woman can move her brains as well as her tail and makes a talented conversationalist. The Angora Woman will spin a magic love spell on you.

Finicky Feline

Ms. Angora has a strange fascination with anything to do with water. When taking a romantic stroll through the park, don't be alarmed if she leaps into a fountain and splashes around. Be a sport—join her!

Cat's Meow

As long as you build a workout room where she can keep in shape and rehearse her fancy feline dance moves, the Angora Woman will remain a content kitten.

Bombay

Personality

The Bombay Babe is a looker! Most men are mesmerized at first glance by her sleek and striking appearance. The trick here is finding a way to meet this elusive creature. Ms. Bombay spends most of her time indoors and more than likely works from home as well. She's a peaceful soul who detests loud noises and crowds. If you're fortunate enough to be introduced and then to date the Bombay Woman, get ready for a loving but somewhat low-key courtship. Longevity within this union will depend on whether you're a man who is over the hoopla and ready for a family.

Finicky Feline

The Bombay Woman will show her claws if she thinks her man isn't giving her enough quality time and attention. She can be possessive if neglected!

Cat's Meow

One of the most endearing qualities about Ms. Bombay is that she'll eagerly give her man praise when he pleases her.

Burmese

Personality
Ms. Burmese will make you weak in your knees—literally, men, if you're not in excellent physical condition. The Burmese Woman is athletic, social, and always on the go! She'll spend time during her daily workweek at the gym, her nightly party schedule will be full, and weekends are made for long countryside jogs. Tired yet? Let's hope not—because soon you'll have to pack your bags to go on a trip with the worldly Ms. Burmese. She enjoys travel, new environments, and fresh conversations with fascinating strangers. Remember, that's how she met you!

Finicky Feline
If you pussyfoot around and don't take the initiative, or you just can't keep up with the Burmese Woman, she'll find a man who can! She bores quickly.

Cat's Meow
You're probably thinking that this woman is too busy to settle down. Not true! Ms. Burmese makes the perfect soccer mom—she'll probably even referee!

European Shorthair

Personality

Hey, guys, when you first meet the expressive European Shorthair Woman, you'll think she's an open book by the wide-eyed look on her face. Not so. Her majestic and strong presence stems from her European ancestors surviving centuries of weather changes, plagues, and wars. She is an aloof thinker. Ms. Euro Chic is an independent gal who likes to spend time reading, watching thought-provoking movies, visiting museums, or volunteering for her favorite political cause—by herself. Then again, she can be playful when challenged with well-thought-out games designed to amuse her! As long as the European Shorthair Woman can rely on a regular schedule with you, including dinners and socializing, she'll feel secure enough to let you both enjoy separate interests. This cultured and sophisticated woman is a firm believer in keeping her man on a comfortably long leash.

Finicky Feline

The European Shorthair Woman is extremely intolerant of tomcats who chase every queen in town. She's territorial and not above a good old-fashioned catfight when another feline encroaches on her marital turf.

Cat's Meow

This gal is healthy and robust! The European Shorthair Woman has incredible stamina and will keep up with every twist and turn you take in life.

Himalayan

Personality

Ms. Himalayan loves to be a-playin'. Guys, if you want a woman who's a real character and will keep you guessing throughout your years together, look no farther! The Himalayan Woman can be a contradiction of sorts: one minute intelligently inquisitive and the next minute gentle and demure. Ms. Himalayan will take her professional career seriously. And when you do decide to marry or cohabitate, her ambition doesn't stop at home. She's a handywoman. Whether it's planting a garden, fixing the plumbing, or building a new nursery addition to your loving abode, the Himalayan Woman will be right by your side and assisting in all the details!

Finicky Feline

The Himalayan Woman's known curiosity can get the best of her if she doesn't learn to channel her energy. Encourage her to streamline all the projects she has in the kitty!

Cat's Meow

If you unintentionally slight Ms. Himalayan, she will call you on it. But she is truly forgiving and won't hold a grudge. In her heart, she knows you both have more important things to do!

Maine Coon

Personality

When the majestic main squeeze Maine Coon queen greets you with a big hug, you'll feel it. She's a tall, strong, muscular woman with a healthy intellect as well. Although most men are considered the hunters in a relationship, Ms. Maine Coon thrives on being a talented pursuer. Men, indulge her and rally a fun game of cat and mouse, preferably in an outdoor setting. You certainly won't mind when the Maine Coon Woman catches you. If she's the one, this would be the most opportune time to surprise her by popping the question. Ms. Maine Coon will coo, as she truly desires to get married and have a family.

Finicky Feline

Ms. Maine Coon has the peculiar habit of sleeping in unusual places at any given time. Don't be shocked when you find her sleeping outside in a hammock during the middle of a snow shower. The natural elements don't faze her.

Cat's Meow

The Maine Coon Woman has an amusing side and has been known to diffuse tense situations with the right play on words at the perfect moment. And isn't timing everything?

Manx

Personality

Okay, men—remember that looks aren't everything. So what if Ms. Maverick Manx doesn't have a prominent tail? She's still an unusual beauty, so cut her some slack. The Manx Woman is loyal beyond belief and will be your staunchest supporter. She'll defend you as long as she's your main attraction. The Manx Lady loves to be part of a dynamic duo. Motherhood suits her, as she blossoms when her home is full of lively activity. As time goes by, Ms. Manx might be a candidate for the empty-litter syndrome—so plan ahead and try to retire early. Oh, and set your watch alarm for 10:30 PM; Ms. Manx gets a nightly second wind around this time, and she'll jump from a quiet lap cat to an energized wild tiger in a split second.

Finicky Feline

Ms. Manx doesn't like surprises. Please don't bring the guys home unexpectedly for an impromptu football party. This will make her very nervous and upset!

Cat's Meow

Although the Manx prefers the tranquil home life, she's been known to be a competitive hunter in the corporate jungle if the need arises.

Ocicat

Personality

The spotted Ocicat is where it's at! This wild-looking woman appears to be unattainable, as if she just walked out of some mysterious jungle. Take heart, men. Although Ms. Ocicat portrays the air of the unknown, she actually thinks of herself as one of the guys. The Ocicat Woman is friendly and outgoing and feels right at home with both men and women. She possesses a unique feline formula consisting of playfulness, independence, and complete dedication to her man. The Ocicat Woman is the quintessential career gal. Her adaptability to new surroundings, outgoing nature, and love of work and travel leave her unchallenged in the entrepreneurial arena. Not to worry; she'll find more than enough hours in the day for you! The Ocicat Woman will hang on your every word with complete sincerity, heartfelt curiosity, and pure admiration. Are *you* purring yet?

Finicky Feline

The Ocicat Woman can be overly possessive of her toys, including her favorite plaything—her man.

Cat's Meow

Ms. Ocicat is one fun gal! Her athletic constitution combined with her comical sense of humor can make for some real slapstick moments on the tennis court and golf course; she may even sign you up for a couples' survival reality show.

Persian

Personality

The purring Persian Woman is a content kitten at heart.
She demands respect and kindness from the man who pursues
her, and from his friends too. The Persian Lady is a loving,
affectionate, and socially adept partner. Just because she's
unassuming doesn't mean she won't jump on the opportunity to
travel when the chance arrives. Any man would be honored to
have her on his arm, as she shines when on show. The one key
to remember when planning your romantic trysts with Ms.
Persian is to make sure that you schedule enough time for daily
catnaps and pampering. She needs her beauty sleep.

Finicky Feline

Even though the Persian Woman has a naturally composed
demeanor, don't try to rub her fur the wrong way just to get a
rise out of her. This lady does have a temper, and she'll let you
know when to back off.

Cat's Meow

The Persian Woman gives as good as she gets. If you're
attentive and you lavish her with gifts, laughter, and love,
she'll return the gestures tenfold.

Ragdoll

Personality

If you're an old-fashioned type of man who still believes in chivalry and protecting his woman from the harsh world, then the relaxed Ragdoll Woman is your queen. This California dreamer is the most docile and laid-back woman around. Ms. Ragdoll abhors confrontation and would rather hide than partake in a catfight. Therefore, it's obvious that she prefers the quiet and cozy country life or the beach to the rush and abrasiveness of the city. One of Ms. Ragdoll's most endearing qualities is that when she's held, she totally relaxes and goes limp. It's as if within your arms she's found the eternal calm she's been seeking in the storm. Chances are that Ms. Ragdoll doesn't want to work unless it's a profession in which she doesn't have to deal with others. Her sensitive nature prohibits her from venturing far from home or dealing with the masses. The Ragdoll Woman is a "puppycat" who expects her man to be the provider. Are you up to the task?

Finicky Feline

Men, you can't always be there to fight Ms. Ragdoll's battles. Less sensitive souls might take advantage of her gentle nature and exploit her frailties. Encourage her to toughen up and show her claws more often.

Cat's Meow

When you arrive home after a long, hectic day at work, you'll be entering your own tranquil paradise with Ms. Ragdoll there to please and soothe you!

Rex

Personality

Hey, guys, the Rex Woman might seem like a gentle creature when you first meet her, but she's full of fun and games. Ms. Rambunctious Rex is a no-nonsense type of gal and will do what it takes to get what she wants. Once she's set her sights on you, she's intelligent and mischievous enough to win you over before you're aware of what happened. Now that the cat is out of the bag, revel in the fact that Ms. Rex chose you as her prey! The Rex Woman is excellent marriage material and a creatively active mother. Life won't be boring with this woman, as she'll devise new schemes to keep you interested.

Finicky Feline

Here we go, men. This is a touchy subject for most women, but you'll have to address the fact that Ms. Rex tends to overeat and gain weight easily. She'll keep svelte by eating several small portions and working out daily.

Cat's Meow

The Rex Woman is a domestic diva who adores the home life. With her, there is the promise of a bountiful life with love, children, and spontaneous shenanigans sure to keep you on your toes!

Russian Blue

Personality

How to woo the Russian Blue? Gentlemen only need apply. The Russian Blue Lady is quiet and shy and doesn't take kindly to brash, aggressive advances. But if you're a man who is reserved and enjoys quiet, romantic dinners at a cozy restaurant and candlelit evenings at home, this is your dream girl! The Russian Blue Woman is a peaceful homebody who blossoms under the comfort of a secure, loving lifestyle. She's 100 percent marriage material and is revered for being an attentive mother. Make sure the heat is on or move to a warm climate when you decide to purchase your private castle together. The Russian Blue Woman is genetically conditioned to catch cold easily, as her ancestors had to brave the subartic temperatures together in Russia.

Finicky Feline

Don't let Ms. Russian Blue make a hermit out of you! It's safe to say that you might have to coach and introduce this woman to the fine art of entertaining at home.

Cat's Meow

Although Ms. Russian Blue might appear too bashful to play, engage her and you'll be pleasantly surprised at her silly side!

Scottish Fold

Personality

Lo and behold the unique Scottish Fold! The Scottish Fold Woman has been referred to as a real doll! She has the expression of a beautiful mannequin with very unusual ears! Men, don't let this frighten you away! Ms. Scottish Fold is quite authentic and all woman. Upon first meeting her, some unknowing people might think she's a bit haughty. Au contraire, it's just that she's more reserved and prefers to be sure she's on safe footing before opening up. Ms. Scottish Fold is a true lady and is selective about with whom, when, and where she shares her love. The key to capturing the Scottish Fold Woman's heart is that she secretly desires love and attention. Ms. Scottish Fold isn't cold or bold; she just wants a home and a man to hold!

Finicky Feline

The Scottish Fold Woman's Achilles' heel is her sensitivity about her ears. Yes, her look is rare and distinct, but that's what sets her apart from the rest. Remind her of this again and again.

Cat's Meow

Your Scottish Fold ladylove makes a delightful mother. You can expect her to instill both discipline and play in your litter.

Siamese

Personality

Have you been working out at the gym lately? Let's hope so, because this exotic beauty is going to keep you on your toes. Ms. Siamese, if you please, is quite the vocalist and will raise her voice with relentless meowing to get her point across. She's a talker, yapper, and nonstop communicator. Please don't walk away or ignore her when she feels misunderstood, because this tactic won't work and she won't let up. She loves to socialize and entertain at home as much as possible; the more the merrier. Don't worry, guys, that this extroverted feline might elusively give you the slip. The Siamese Woman is one of the only cats that can be leashed.

Finicky Feline

The Siamese Woman can experience extreme mood swings and behave erratically. One day she'll be playful, lighthearted, and fun, and the next day you might find her sulking without any reason. Oh, and by the way, she does have a jealous streak, so it would behoove you not to flirt with any other women at Ms. Siamese's famous soirees.

Cat's Meow

Ms. Siamese is very affectionate and demonstrative; if you reciprocate, you'll both be happy! She's changeable, men, so you'll have to be ready to read her, knowing when to give her a hug and when to give her space.

Siberian

Personality

The sweet Siberian Woman is a well-rounded creature. Ms. Siberian will patiently wait to greet you at the front door; then she'll sit you down, jump on your lap, and ask you about your day. She's a ball of energy and will cater to your every whim, even joyfully bringing you breakfast in bed on weekends, with all your favorites. Men, the Siberian Woman is totally hooked and curious about computers and won't hesitate to add her two cents when you're working on a project. Don't be shocked to find a few unexpected but accurate lines added to your monthly board members presentation, courtesy of Ms. Siberian, of course. It's her way of being helpful and contributing to your common good—your future together—which, by the way, includes a house with a white picket fence and lots of little Siberians.

Finicky Feline

You'll encounter a problem with Ms. Siberian if you're the type of man who relishes lots of solo time. She will insist on constantly being with you and assisting with everything—even reading the morning newspaper.

Cat's Meow

The Siberian Woman knows intuitively when something is upsetting you. She will nurse you back to health mentally, physically, and emotionally, each and every time.

Somali

Personality

Does the Somali Woman love you—or love you not? This is the question you'll be toying with over and over again. But won't you have lots of fun mulling over the answer! The Somali Woman is a contradiction; she's shy and cautious with people and at the same time fearless when pursuing her freedom. Where do you fit in to this equation? Somewhere in the middle! Ms. Somali has a mistrustful approach to love, and it's going to take some true romancing, wining and dining, and gifts and trips before she fully reveals herself. Once she does, your cuddly lap cat is affectionate and demonstrative. Please don't take it personally when she calls you on Friday night and tells you she's leaving for some bargain hunting in another state. This woman loves her space! Besides, she'll bring you back a thoughtful gift. Ahhh, see? She does love you!

Finicky Feline

The Somali Woman has the curious habit of mimicking the expression of those she admires. When you take Ms. Somali out for dinner and it seems as if you're dating a mirror, be flattered and make some clever funny faces. You'll both have a good laugh.

Cat's Meow

Within the Somali Woman's quirkiness lies her beauty. This woman is unpredictable, mysterious, affectionate, and playful—all wrapped up in one neat package. Hint to all men: Keeping you guessing is half her fun.

Stray or Rescued Cat

Personality

Some men like to play the role of knight in shining armor, and this woman might be your perfect damsel in distress. This complex woman is a mix of being comfortable on her own, being naturally self-sufficient, and at the same time wanting a home to call her own. The man that falls for this woman will have to be patient with her. She's led a solo life until she met him, possibly roaming as a gypsy from home to home, street to street, city to city, even country to country. Trust will have to be built. When this worldly woman pulls out her bagpipes and plays an Irish tune, then recites Sartre's philosophies on life, simultaneously talking about the latest in politics, you'll find her an exciting woman and will want to embrace the many facets of her personality. Ultimately, this woman wants a home to share with a secure and caring companion. She desires a cozy place, good meals, and warm arms.

Finicky Feline

Trust will be an issue here! This stray siren hasn't led a very secure life but has a lot to offer. Once she's found a safe haven with a man who accepts her unconditionally, she'll gradually unfold and blossom into the loving cat she's always desired to be.

Cat's Meow

Once you penetrate the protective emotional walls Ms. Rescued has constructed, you'll find a heart of pure gold. Don't forget to be gentle and patient when she hides because she's feeling lost or insecure.

Tonkinese

Personality

Whether Ms. Tonkinese is twenty years old or fifty, she'll exude an adventuresome nature with a curious mind. The Tonkinese tomboy is young at heart and loves the arts! She flourishes in the limelight and will probably choose a profession in the entertainment industry. What she wants in a man is a true pal and a partner who will accompany her on all her star-studded escapades. One caveat in this dreamy romantic scenario is that she is messy! If you're a man with a domestic side, then move in with or marry the Tonkinese Woman, and beam with pride.

Finicky Feline

Hey, men—keep your financial records, diary, and confidential papers under lock and key! The Tonkinese Woman isn't necessarily nosy; it's just that she wants to know everything about the man she loves!

Cat's Meow

Where's the party? Ms. Tonkinese is the quintessential hostess and will gladly invite your entire family and friends over for Sunday brunch and holiday dinners.

CHAPTER THREE

Cat Colors

"The smallest feline is a masterpiece."

Leonardo da Vinci

D oes your Lady Luck own a black or white feline, and will this affect your future fortunes? Is she highly superstitious? If the love of your life chooses a tabby cat, what does it say about her personality and temperament? This color-coated chapter will assist you with fine-tuning your understanding of the woman you cohabitate with, date, or work beside by the coloring of the cat(s) she shares her life with. It's a proven fact that color has a strong influence on which cat a woman picks—so read on!

Black-Cat Woman

The mysterious black-cat woman has had a lot said and written about her over the years. You'd have to be from another planet not to have heard the superstitions attached to black cats. So what does it mean if your woman owns a black cat? First of all, it depends on where she was born. In Britain and Japan, it's actually a good omen if a black cat crosses your path, whereas in the United States and several other European countries, it's not a very fortunate sign. She will bring you good luck if she greets you at the front door, but if you're repainting the ceiling, kindly ask her to walk around the ladder you're standing on instead of underneath it, just in case some of the negative folklore holds true. The laid-back black-cat woman (say that quickly five times!) is extremely loyal, stubborn, and naturally suspicious of strangers. Keep a close eye on her, as she enjoys getting lost in the moment and wandering off (mixed-black-cat women tend to be more sociable and friendly). Halloween will be her favorite celebration, so why not get into the spirit and fun of the festivities by dressing up as her canine nemesis?

White-Cat Woman

Just like her polar opposite, the black cat, the white cat has had many myths and superstitions created around her. If you dream about your white-cat woman at night or unexpectedly drive by her walking down the street during the day, ask for a raise at work or play the lottery; American folklore claims it's a sign of good luck. A white cat's fur is the purest (the result of a gene that suppresses color), and this is why your white-cat woman's temperament, in addition to her heart, is true, calm, and peaceful. Don't be fooled by her low-key demeanor and expect her to be a stay-at-home wife and mother. She will like to have a good time periodically and can be extremely friendly, inviting the neighbors over for an impromptu party when the mood strikes her. The white-cat woman might appear timid (mixed-white-cat women are more timid), even nervous, but will surprise you by her streetwise comments, common sense, and desire to take off into the wild blue yonder—without you! She'll return a wiser pussycat, quietly narrating her latest adventure, like a magical bedtime story, to you before you go to sleep at night, until you're tranquilly purring again.

Black-and-White-Cat Woman

This Zen black-and-white-cat woman has brought the yin and the yang together in her personality, which creates an even-tempered temptress. She might appear to be a bit too easygoing for her own good, but remember: She has found her center and she'll be a calm, welcome sounding board when life throws a curveball or two your way. This black-and-white cookie of a cat is quite approachable and makes friends easily, and like her black-cat and white-cat cousins, she has been known to take off on spontaneous escapades when the cry of the wild calls. Cats always revisit the place where they're fed, and since you're the man feeding her soul, you don't have to worry that she'll find your replacement. If you dream of the black-and-white woman while dozing off waiting for her to return, this is a positive omen meaning luck with children and the birth of a child—possibly your own?

Red- or Ginger-Cat Woman

The ginger-cat woman is true to her redhead reputation: fiery and full of vigor! Her ancestry started back in Asia but spread through Scotland, Ireland, and Europe—thanks to the Vikings. She's a hot commodity, as the ginger males outnumber the ginger females three to one. Let's hope that a little competition won't thwart your efforts to win her heart, because this ball of fire is worth the fight. The ginger-cat woman can be spirited and sly, and isn't above coaxing you to prove your loyalty and affections for her by a valiant act of chivalry. If you're a man who doesn't mind a modern-day duel (a verbal one through e-mail, for instance), then go ahead and accept the challenge. She'll be highly impressed by your passion. The ginger-cat woman wants action and might get annoyed when bored or irritated. Beware of this cat when that happens and try to appease her. She's known to have a temper and she'll take out her claws to get her point across!

Blue- or Gray-Cat Woman

The beautiful blue-cat woman is a gentle soul. Her charming and graceful demeanor will pull you in the minute you meet her. Right from the start you'll want to get close to the blue-cat woman as you sense her warmth and caring nature. Don't hesitate to show your appreciation for her by loving acts of affection and appreciation. She will reciprocate in kind and let you know that you're the focus of her heart. Ms. Blue isn't too good to be true. If you're waiting for her to turn into a ferocious feline, it's not going to happen. She's a calm and peaceful lady (especially if she's a mixed blue). Her ancestors weathered the freezing temperatures in Russia, and that may be why she would rather bask in the glow of a loving relationship than in the chill of being alone.

Calico-Cat Woman

The very healthy calico-cat woman is the quintessential feline. She actually belongs to an exclusive Women-Cats-Only club. The calico-cat woman loves to dress in three colors at one time, most noticeably, orange, white, and red or cream—and sometimes shades of black, blue, chocolate, lilac, cinnamon, or fawn. Now you know what color outfit to buy her when picking out a birthday or special-occasion gift. This exciting woman can swing from dancing all night at a nightclub to daydreaming on a hammock, from quietly watching a romantic movie with you to engaging in a four-hour-long intellectual conversation concerning world affairs. If you're an entrepreneur starting out in your own business for the first time, the calico-cat woman might just be your good-luck charm. In Japan, it's believed that this woman will bring you money and riches. Overall, the calico-cat woman is good-natured (mixed are a bit more feisty). If you add marriage, a home, and children to your love equation, you might just have it all with this colorful lady!

Tortoiseshell-Cat Woman

The tortoiseshell-cat woman is commonly nicknamed Naughty Tortie. Curious yet? She can be hot tempered and full of life all at the same time (especially the mixed torties). Figuring out this woman is going to be like putting the pieces of a jigsaw puzzle together. Just when you think she might be too hot for you to handle, she'll do an about-face and become compassionate and loving. You'll also be pleasantly surprised at her natural maternal side, which you'll get to witness firsthand when your niece and nephew visit during a school vacation. The tortoise-shell-cat woman is also known for her quick-witted repartee and will have you in stitches at one of her famous quips. Let's see; the woman of your dreams is passionate, loving, marriage and mother material, and funny! Looks like the complicated pieces of your love puzzle are actually designed to bring you a life full of entertaining bliss with the tortoiseshell-cat woman!

Tabby-Cat Woman

The home-loving tabby-cat woman makes her abode a welcoming and cozy jungle. She prefers to decorate her home with lots of plants, relaxing hiding places fluffed with camouflage pillows, and lots of open window space. The tabby-cat woman dislikes crowds and would rather have close friends and family over to her place instead of venturing out. She has refined her hostess and social skills and you'll be proud of her when you entertain together. The main problem you'll find when dating or living with the sweet tabby-cat woman is that she gets so relaxed indoors that she might begin to add on the pounds and languish from inactivity (mixed have an even greater tendency toward this). It's your job as her partner and as an act of love to encourage her to work out more often. Sit down and design a jungle-themed exercise room tailor-made for both of you, and join her in a daily routine. Not only will your feline feel svelte, but she'll also receive a cat confirmation about your loyalty and devotion!

CHAPTER FOUR

How to Live with a Cat Woman

"The phrase 'domestic cat' is an oxymoron."
GEORGE F. WILL

From catnip to kitty litter, a man has to be knowledgeable and equipped to incorporate into his daily routine the requirements of his feline counterpart. He has to be aware of the feminine wiles in his regal cat-mosphere, and avoid *cat*-astrophe by catering to and comprehending them all. If his girlfriend, wife, or cat gently nudges him, does this mean she feels ignored and wants more attention? Since all cats love catnip, find the special nip that your woman craves. It might be chocolates, perfume, flowers, fancy feasts, or a romantic walk on the beach. To keep her in a happy mood, spoil her with her favorite treats!

Kitty-Litter-Box Cleaning

One of the most unpleasant realities when living with your woman and her cat is the infamous cat-litter box. Since it should be cleaned at least once a week, for the obvious hygienic reasons, you're going to have to be a real man, brave it, roll up your sleeves, and do the dirty deed. Empty the litter box! Now, in all fairness, it's only right that you and your girlfriend, wife, or lover take turns sharing in this domestic responsibility. Trust me; making a proactive effort in this cohabitating department will be truly appreciated by the entire household, especially by your grateful kitty. FYI, baking powder helps with cat-litter-box odor. There are even electronic litter boxes on the market—all you have to do is press a little button to start the cleaning process.

The Catnip Connection

When you first meet the cat(s) of the woman you're dating, one sure way to win instant approval is to bring catnip. Catnip acts as a feel-good antidote for most cats and is

found at pet stores everywhere. This small offering will work wonders in making a good first impression on the feline(s). But the effects do wear off, and your real intentions and personality will leave the lasting mark. The same holds true for the woman you're dating, living with, or married to. You can buy her as many gifts and tokens of affection as you

want, but there's much truth to the old saying that "money can't buy you love"—although it can help. Men, understand that women are attracted to shiny, pretty things in small boxes and are truly thankful for gifts. But ultimately what they want is priceless: love, respect, devotion, friendship, appreciation, and honesty—a soul mate that can go the distance of a lifetime.

Grooming Gorgeous

Cats are clean creatures by nature and feel as good as they look. Each breed of cat has different grooming requirements, and it's important for their basic happiness that their needs are attended to. Each breed of woman isn't much different.

Some cats and women are outdoorsy, low-maintenance felines, while others are long-haired, indoor, high-maintenance creatures. It all depends on the unique personality traits of each breed, men! When living with a woman and her cat(s), you must get involved with their overall lifestyle! Build your physically active cats a specially designed cat section in an open room. If your ladylove is high energy,

sign her up at a gym, buy her a workout video, or create an exercise room in your home. Let's say the premiere felines in your life are high maintenance and prefer pampering and napping. Then brush your cats' fur, check their teeth weekly, and use olive oil on the eye area when required (as with all domestic cats). Send your wife or girlfriend to a spa for a massage and skin-treatment session, or even better yet—send her off on a shopping spree. With just a little effort on your part, both felines will be smiling like Cheshire cats, feeling fine and relaxed, and purring at your feet.

One Crowded Bed

It's a well-known fact that a good night's sleep is important when it comes to our daily performance levels, health restoration, and overall temperament. And it's also widely known that cats are nocturnal creatures. Men, you can't blame them; their ancestral genetic code was programmed to hunt vermin at night, long before exterminators took on the job. When you're newly cohabitating with a woman and her cat(s), get ready for some restless nights, especially if you're a light sleeper—and on full moons, when the hunt will be intensified. Your dream woman will also feel friskier and more playful when the moon is totally waxed. You might suggest that your girlfriend or wife's cat sleep outside your bedroom, but this might not be feasible if the cat has been sleeping on the bed since it was a kitten. If the meowing doesn't keep you up at night, then the scratching at the door to get back in the bedroom will! Some cats look for a warm place to rest, particularly when temperatures cool down. Although napping during the day is part of a cat's schedule (resting up for the evening pursuit), more interaction and playing with your cat daily might tire your feline's ferociousness and quell the nighttime

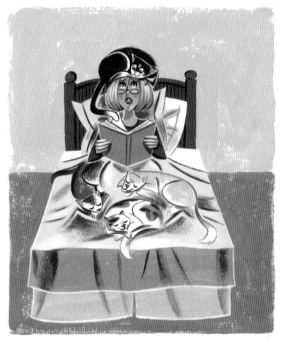

meanderings. And if that doesn't do the trick, then leave the bedroom door open at night so your cat(s) can leave at will, try using the command No, and/or just accept your fate and buy a bigger bed!

Amorous Attention

A woman will let you know in her own way when she wants your attention, just like her cat counterpart. The trick here is

that you might not know exactly when this will happen with your girlfriend or wife. A cat will meow, rub up against your leg, or butt heads when it needs a few extra strokes. The woman in your life will have her own special cat cry. Guys, your job is to be astute to both the subtle meows and blatantly obvious ploys for your affection, as each breed of woman is different. One woman will call and e-mail obsessively, while another will play hard-to-reach by refusing to answer her phone or e-mails, simply to incite your curiosity and lure you into her den. The bolder gal will verbally let you know in no uncertain terms that neglect is not her thing and she wants attention now! Another darling dame will shower you with sweet nothings and kind gestures to get you to acquiesce to her desires. Remember, men, the key to your united happiness is that women, like cats, are changeable, independent, and unpredictable, and it will be up to you to be able to read the signs when your woman wants some good old-fashioned loving!

Savior Scratching Post

Cats can't help it! Keeping their claws sharp is a natural part of their instinctive nature. When newly living with or married to a woman, you must take note of what type of cat she owns before moving in all your furniture. Lucky you if your cat ventures outside for excitement. There it will find a tree or wooden post on which to scratch and sharpen its claws. But that prize, custom-made sofa and the matching carpet you ordered from a European antique dealer might look more like a prime scratching post to your indoor domestic cat when it gets the itch to scratch! Men, if your girlfriend or wife doesn't

already have a scratching post, do yourself a huge favor and avoid any aggravation and arguments by purchasing one (or several, depending on the number of cats in the household) immediately. This one simple piece of wood will be your saving grace and will help you avoid catching a nasty case of cat-scratch fever. Some owners clip their cats' claws themselves, but this is a very tricky and difficult process and it's better to consult a groomer or vet to perform the procedure. Some animal lovers and professionals consider declawing cats to be cruel. Especially if a cat gets lost or escapes, having been declawed can prove dangerous. Cats need their claws for hunting, climbing, and fighting enemies. Listen, fellas, the woman in your life needs her claws taken care of too. Treat her to a manicure or pedicure before she takes a turn at your furniture (wink-wink).

Annoying Allergies

Here's a real cat conundrum. You meet the woman of your dreams and she invites you back to her place for a nightcap; there she introduces you to her cat. Before your second sip of wine, you're wheezing and sneezing, and your eyes are swelling up like a couple of red balloons. Not the romantic scenario you envisioned! Unfortunately, you're probably allergic to her cat. Before you curse Cupid, get an allergy test to indeed find out whether you're allergic to your girlfriend's cat and not some other household environmental allergen. If your cat allergy is confirmed, there are several steps you and your ladylove can take to alleviate your symptoms. It might be a true testimony of love if your girlfriend agrees to bathe her cat every four to six weeks to remove the dandruff from under the skin that often causes most allergic reactions. You might have to convince her to get rid of any carpets and synthetic fabrics that hold dust and dander more than natural fabrics. Buy your dream date an air purifier as a practical gift to place in her home, and remind her that it will help you breathe easier, so you'll be able to stay over

longer. And since you don't want to seem like more of a job than a pleasure, offer to help clean her bedspreads, pillows, and rugs and then take turns vacuuming. There is one very lucky perk to being allergic to cats—you never have to clean the litter box! If all of the above tips don't help you, consult with your physician, as there are homeopathic and prescription medications you can take to ease your pain. Are you both still in love? Your girlfriend will admire your labor of love and your efforts will bring you closer!

CHAPTER FIVE

Cat Lady One . . . Two . . . Three . . .

"One cat just leads to another."

ERNEST HEMINGWAY

What's a man to do if he's dating, living with, or married to a woman that owns one or more cats? This chapter will provide you with the distinct personalities of women who are the queen cats in households of one, two, three—up to six felines. Men, you'll learn what to expect from each Cat Lady . . . and how to acclimate to your woman's cat lair. Let's get started.

Cat Lady One

With Cat Lady One, expect to have singular fun! This woman is very comfortable with one-to-one relationships. She probably chose one cat because she prefers the closeness of having just one other living thing to lavish her attention on. This will apply to other areas of her life, including romance, career, friendships, and social life. A primary focal point and streamlined thinking are apt to be just two of her strong points. She will feel quite content spending most of her free time at home and working from there also. Cat Lady One likes to keep life simple and uncomplicated. Now, when you enter the picture, the household pecking order is going to change and compound the complexity of the living situation. It's important that your beloved's cat doesn't feel that you're intruding on its territory. Remember, this cat is slightly spoiled, numero uno, and not used to sharing its coveted love throne. Set up a scheduled time to play with this coddled cat to curtail any feelings of feline jealousy. Regularly bring some catnip and toys over, and create a specially tailored game. Before you know it, the two of you will be great friends and living harmoniously with Cat Lady One.

Cat Lady Two

With Cat Lady Two, there will be more time for you! When you're dating or living with a woman with two cats, you can expect her to feel free to socialize with you and leave the cats alone, because they can keep each other company. This woman is compassionate and has realized that it would be far better for all concerned if her cats had companionship of the same kind. Her twosome mind-set allows her the freedom and the space to pursue other activities outside the home without an overwhelming sense of guilt. Cat Lady Two is bound to have a career and outside interests, such as going to the gym or to night classes to enhance her professional status. This doesn't mean that she loves her animals any less, and by all means don't assume she won't be spending time with them; she will be (and so will you)! Actually, when you're at home with your ladylove, expect to be mutually lavishing her cats with attention and enjoying many of the shenanigans they schemed while the two of you were out to dinner. Cat Lady Two and you will share dual responsibilities and laughs!

Cat Lady Three

With Cat Lady Three, you'll need more than one scratching post or tree! Life becomes a bit more complicated when you're dating or living with a woman who owns three or more cats. Cat Woman Three is a multifaceted lady who thrives on constant activity and a plenitude of interests. She has a wide circle of friends who are bent on humanitarian causes and services. Her professional choice will be one that utilizes her many talents, especially if she can work as a business consultant with various creative clients and projects. Your ladylove will want you to be able to capture her mentally and keep her feeling alive romantically. Now, when you start to date or live with this woman, there are a few safeguards that need to be put in place to keep the peace and avoid daily catfights. Your first feline father job is to make sure that there is more than one kitty-litter box; otherwise, the cats will be jockeying for position and getting feisty when they have to wait. This also saves you from having to clean up "outside the box." *Note:* If one cat dominates in your household, the other cats might become irritated and start to scratch your furniture, sharpening their claws for the obvious impending fight for supremacy. Save yourself a lot of anxiety by purchasing a few scratching posts or trees; then strategically place them around your home. You and Cat Lady Three will never feel alone!

Cat Lady Four

With Cat Lady Four, leave open the back door! Here's one organized and accomplished lady. How else would she be able to afford and run a household with four cats? Cat Lady Four is a master planner who has thoughtful foresight when it comes to long-range goals and probably calculated you into the scheme of things long before you did. You're just one big tomcat, right? This woman is astute and skilled enough to realize that everything has its place, cats and you included. Romantically she behaves in a similar structured fashion. She doesn't like to play any games (except with her cats) and prefers a man who is serious, committed, and as goal oriented as she is. Now, living with Cat Lady Four is going to be a lesson in discipline. When it comes to feeding time, you're going to resemble a top chef in a cat restaurant with four prime tables to attend to. Each cat should have its own steel or ceramic (plastic retains smells) food and water dish carefully placed in different dining areas in your home. And since cats have varied eating habits, from inhaling their entire meal in one giant lick to taking small, grazing bites throughout the day, the farther apart (even selected elevations) the designated eating areas are—all the better! It might make life easier if you convince your girlfriend or wife to consider letting the cats go outside for some au naturel extracurricular activities.

When considering buying a house or an apartment together, make sure you have a backyard—and a back-door flap through which the cats can enter and exit at will. If you add a little spontaneity to the equation, Cat Lady Four will adore you even more!

Cat Lady Five

With Cat Lady Five you'll be responsible for more than nine lives! At first you might think it's out of the ordinary for one woman to possess as much energy as she does. There has to be something wrong with her, right? Not so. Cat Lady Five was born with a high-energy gene that branches out into every area of her life. That's why you shouldn't be shocked when you enter her home for the first time and count not just one, two, three, or four—but five—felines. She prides herself on having enough love to give and more. Actually, this lady thrives on motivating action and positive chaos, and her five cats act like little muses that fuel her already high-octane levels. Don't worry that this woman won't find the time for you; she will. Life won't be boring with Cat Lady Five. She'll have you entertained by running to the newest movie and then to the oldest antique show in just one afternoon. Her love of activity flows throughout her personal and romantic life as well (wink-wink). Living with this woman is going to take some observant cat exploration and research on your part. Cats are sociable and create a hierarchy among themselves when living under the same roof. Your job will be to understand each cat's individual placement in the pecking order and act accordingly. It will help you to build a structured territorial environment for the entire gang, including you.

Construct personal window perches, scratching trees on different levels for the five felines, and a special, cozy hiding place for the low kitty on the totem pole, who will want to run and hide periodically. Place their individual feeding bowls by each designated territory and simultaneously gain control of what could otherwise become a free-for-all household. Cat Lady Five will be turned on by your take-charge attitude toward her and the entire cat crew!

Cat Lady Six

With Cat Lady Six, make sure her cats are fixed! When dating or living with Cat Lady Six, you might feel as if you've taken on the role of a zookeeper or, better yet, Tarzan, King of the Jungle. But what makes your queen of the jungle tick? This woman is totally maternal and nurturing. Whenever friends call and ask her to take in a stray or rescued cat, she doesn't have it in her heart to turn them down. Cat Lady Six can't even begin to think about an "underdog" cat that's down on its luck being left out in the cold or even worse—destroyed because no one cared. She considers the entire animal kingdom (humans included) as one big interconnected family that should be provided with the basics: shelter, food, water, and when possible, love. Her humanitarian approach to life will apply to you as well. Men, she will always make sure that you're taken care of by being an attentive and present partner. Lucky you! Please read all the other Cat Lady sections to give you insight to living with this special lady. She has so many cats that it will be of the utmost importance that both of you regularly clean all rugs, couches, sheets, and pillows, and the floor, to get rid of cat hair and dander. Here's a suggestion: If Cat Lady Six comes home one day and suggests a seventh addition to your brood, advocate that either you start a not-for-profit organization to help with the

rising costs and the new wing that will have to be built to house all the cats, or find a group that already exists that she can trust for all the guaranteed new cat candidates. Perhaps even mutually volunteer your services to oversee all her "cat kids." Cat Lady Six will hold you close in her heart for your proactive engagement with such a valuable and worthy cause.

CHAPTER SIX

Places to Rescue Your Perfect Cat

The following is a directory of credible and well-established animal organizations throughout the United States and Puerto Rico. The locations and contact information will aid you in your search for a new feline companion. You should have a keener sense of what cat best suits you after reading the characteristics and personalities of each breed. Whether you're looking for a playful and affectionate kitty, a reserved and dignified lady, or a feline ball of energy, by contacting these organizations you will be sure to find the cat of your dreams. Good luck, and have fun in your quest for that lucky cat!

UNITED STATES

Community Animal
Management
www.saveourstrays.com

Alabama

The Greater Birmingham
Humane Society
300 Snow Dr.
Birmingham, AL 35209
205-942-1211
www.gbhs.org

Humane Society of
Etowah County
1700 Chestnut St.
Gadsden, AL 35901
256-547-4846
humanesocietyetowah-
county.org

Arizona

Arizona Humane Society
1521 W. Dobbins Rd.
Phoenix, AZ 85041
602-997-7586
www.azhumane.org

Humane Society of
Southern Arizona
3540 North Kelvin Blvd.
Tucson, AZ 85716
520-327-6088
www.hssaz.org

Arkansas

Humane Society of
Palaski County
14600 Colonel Glenn Rd.
Little Rock, AR 72210
501-227-6166
www.warmhearts.org

Northeast Arkansas
Humane Society
6111 East Highland Dr.
Jonesboro, AR 72401
870-932-5185
www.neahs.org

California

The Amanda Foundation
310-278-2935
www.amanda-fnd.org

Los Angeles SPCA
5026 W. Jefferson Blvd.
Los Angeles, CA 90016
323 730-5333, ext. 251
888-SPCALA1
www.spcala.org

Much Love Animal
Rescue
P.O. Box 341721
Los Angeles, CA
90034-1721
310-636-9115
www.muchlove.org

San Diego Humane
Society and SPCA
5500 Gaines St.
San Diego, CA 92110
619-299-7012, ext. 2249
www.sdhumane.org

Peninsula Humane
Society and SPCA
12 Airport Blvd.
San Mateo, CA 94401
650-340-7022
http://www.peninsula
humanesociety.org

San Francisco SPCA
2500 16th St.
San Francisco, CA
94103-4213
415-554-3000
www.sfspca.org

Sparky and the Gang
310-364-3668
www.petfinder.org/
shelters/CA270.html
email: sparkyandthe-
gang@excite.com

Colorado

Denver Dumb Friends
League-Humane Society
of Denver—West Shelter
2080 South Quebec St.
Denver, CO 80231
303-696-4941
303-751-5772
http://www.ddfl.org

Connecticut

Connecticut Humane
Society
701 Russell Rd.
Newington, CT 06111
860-594-4500
www.cthumane.org

The Westport Shelter
455 Post Rd. East
Westport, CT 06880-4435
203-227-4137

Delaware

Delaware SPCA
Newcastle County Shelter
455 Stanton
Christiana Rd.
Newark, DE 19713
302-998-2281
www.delspca.org

Florida

Humane Society of
Greater Miami
2101 N.W. 95th St.
Miami, FL 33147
305-696-0800
786-924-5220
www.humane
societymiami.org

South Shelter
16601 SW 117th Ave.
Miami, FL 33177
305-252-3389

Jacksonville Humane
Society
8464 Beach Blvd.
Jacksonville, FL 32216
904-725-8766
www.jaxhumane.org

SPCA of Central Florida
Orlando/Orange
County Shelter
2727 Conroy Rd.
Orlando, FL 32839
407-351-7722
www.ohs-spca.org

Georgia

Atlanta Humane Society
and SPCA
981 Howell Mill Rd.
N.W.
Atlanta, GA 30318-5562
404-875-5331
www.atlhumane.org

Humane Society
Chatham/Savannah
7215 Salle Mood Dr.
Savannah, GA 31406
912-354-9515
www.savannah-
humane.com

Hawaii

Hawaiian Humane
Society
2700 Waialae Ave.
Honolulu, HI 96826
808-946-2187
www.hawaiianhumane.org

Maui Humane Society
Mokulele Hwy.
Pu'unene, HI 96784
808-877-3680
www.mauihumane.org

Idaho

Bannock County Humane
Society
P.O. Box 332
Pocatello, ID 83204
208-232-0371
www.bannockhumane
society.org

Idaho Humane Society
4775 W. Doorman St.
Boise, ID 83705
208-342-3508, ext. 0
www.idahohumane
society.com

Illinois

The Anti-Cruelty Society
510 N. LaSalle
Chicago, IL 60610
312-644-8338
www.anticruelty.org

Chicago Humane
Center—Red Door
P. O. Box 269119
Chicago, IL 60626
773-764-2242
www.reddoorshelter.org

Humane Society of
Central Illinois Pet
Adoption Center
3001 Gill St.
Bloomington, IL
61704-9638
309-664-7387
www.hscipets.org

Paws Chicago
3516 W. 26th St.
Chicago, IL 60623
773-521-1408
www.pawschicago.org

Indiana

Humane Society of
Indianapolis
7929 North Michigan Rd.
Indianapolis, IN 46268
317-872-5650
www.indyhumane.org

The Humane Society of
Jackson County
P.O. Box 135
Seymour, IN 47274
812-522-5200
www.jchumane.org

Kansas

The Humane Society of
Greater Kansas City
5445 Parallel Pkwy.
Kansas City, KS 66104
913-596-1000
www.hsgkc.org

Helping Hands Humane
Society, Inc.
2625 N.W. Rochester Rd.
Topeka, KS 66617-1201
785-233-7325
www.topeka
humaneshelter.org

Kentucky

Kentucky Humane
Society "Lifelong Friends"
241 Steedly Dr.
Louisville, KY 40214
502-366-3355
www.kyhumane.org

Woodford Humane
Society
P.O. Box 44
Versailles, KY 40383
859-873-5491
www.woodfordhumane
society.org

Louisiana

Iberia Humane Society
"Have a Heart"
P.O. Box 11422
New Iberia, LA
70562-1422
318-365-1923
www.iberiahumane.com

St. Tammany Humane
Society
20384 Harrison Ave.
Covington, LA 70433
985-893-9474, ext. 6
985-892-7387
sttammanyhumane-
society.org

New Orleans SPCA
1319 Japonica St.
New Orleans, LA 70117
504-944-7445
www.la-spca.org

Maine

Greater Androscoggin
Humane Society
3312 Hotel Rd.
Auburn, ME 04210
207-783-2311
www.gahumane.org

Humane Society of
Knox County
P.O. Box 1294
Rockland, ME 04841
207-594-2200
www.humanesocietyof-
knoxcounty.org

Maryland

Fredrick County Humane
Society
5712 D Industry Ln.
Frederick, MD 21704
301-694-8300
www.fchs.org

Maryland SPCA
3300 Falls Rd.
Baltimore, MD 21211
410-235-8826
www.mdspca.org

Massachusetts

Animal Rescue League
of Boston
10 Chandler St.
Boston, MA 02116
617-426-9170, ext. 110,
ext. 169
www.arlboston.org

Massachusetts SPCA
350 South
Huntington Ave.
Boston, MA 02130
617-522-7400
www.mspca.org

Northeast Animal Shelter
204 Highland Ave.
P.O. Box 4506
Salem, MA 01970-0901
978-745-9888
www.northeastanimal-
shelter.org

Michigan

Michigan Humane
Society
www.michiganhumane.org

Detroit Shelter
7401 Chrysler Dr.
Detroit, MI 48211
313-872-3400

Rochester Hills Shelter
3600 W. Auburn Rd.
Rochester Hills, MI
48309
248-852-7420

Westland Shelter
37255 Marquette
Westland, MI 48185
734-721-7300

Minnesota

Humane Society for
Companion Animals
1115 Beulah Ln.
St. Paul, MN 55108
651-645-7387
http://www.hsca.net/

Northwoods Humane
Society
9785 Hudson Rd.
Woodbury, MN 55125
651-730-6008
www.northwoodshs.org/

Mississippi

Humane Society of South
Mississippi
Gulfport, MS 39503
228-863-4394
www.hssm.org

Pearl River County
SPCA
P.O. Box 191
Picayune, MS 39466
601-798-8000
www.prcspca.org

Missouri

Animal Protection
Agency
1705 S. Hanley Rd.
Brentwood, MO
63144-2909
314-645-4610, ext. 21

Humane Society of
Missouri St. Louis
Adoption Center
1201 Macklind Ave.
St. Louis, MO 63110
314-951-1562
www.hsmo.org

Westport Area Branch
Adoption Center
2400 Drilling Service Rd.
Maryland Heights, MO
63043
314-951-1588

Montana

Humane Society of
Gallatin Valley
P.O. Box 11390
Bozeman, MT 59719
Email: hsofgv@imt.net

Montana Pets on the Net
Rimrock Humane Society
P.O. Box 834
Roundup, MT 59072
406-323-3687
www.montanapets.org

Nebraska

Central Nebraska
Humane Society
1312 Sky Park Rd.
Grand Island, NE 68801
308-385-5305
members.petfinder.org/
~NE13

Nebraska Humane
Society
8929 Fort St.
Omaha, NE 68134-2899
402-444-7800
www.nehumanesociety.org

Nevada

Nevada Humane Society
200 Kresge Ln.
Sparks, NV 89431
775-434-2009
775-331-5770
www.nevadahumane
society.org

New Hampshire

New Hampshire Humane
Society
1305 Meredith
Center Rd.
Laconia, NH 03246
603-524-3252
www.nhhumane.org

New Jersey

Mt. Pleasant Animal
Shelter
194 Route 10 West
East Hanover, NJ 07936
973-386-0590
www.njshelter.org

New Mexico

Heart and Soul Animal
Sanctuary
369 Montezuma Ave.,
#130
Santa Fe, NM 87501
505-757-6817
www.animal-sanctuary.org

Humane Society of
Taos, Inc.
P.O. Box 622
Taos, NM 87571
505-758-9708
www.joycefay.com/taos/
index.shtml

New York

Animal Rescue Fund of
the Hamptons
P.O. Box 901
Wainscott, NY 11975
631-537-0400
www.arfhamptons.org

ASCPA
424 East 92nd St.
New York, NY 10128
212-876-7700
www.aspca.org

Central New York SPCA
5878 East Molloy Rd.
Syracuse, NY 13211
315-454-4479
www.cnyspca.org

SPCA of Westchester
590 North State Rd.
Briarcliff Manor, NY
10510
914-941-2894
www.spca914.com

Suffolk County SPCA
363 Route 11
Smithtown, NY 11787
631-382-SPCA
www.suffolkspca.org

Green Chimneys
Children's Services and
Green Chimneys School
(featuring human-animal
interactions)
400 Doansburg Rd.,
Box 719
Brewster, NY 10509
845-279-2995
www.greenchimneys.org

Humane Society for
Greater Nashua
24 Ferry Rd.
Nashua, NY 03064-8109
603-889-BARK (2275)
www.hsfn.org

Humane Society of
New York
306 East 59th St.
New York, NY 10022
212-752-4842
www.humanesocietyny.org

Paul Sorvino's DogFellas
212-369-2942
www.dogfellas.net

Stray from the Heart
P.O. Box 11
New York, NY
10024-0011
212-726-DOGS
www.strayfromtheheart.org

North Carolina

Humane Society of
Charlotte
2700 Toomey Ave.
Charlotte, NC 28203
704-377-0534
www.clthumane.org

SPCA of Cumberland
County
3232 Bragg Blvd.
Fayetteville, NC 28303
910-860-1177
www.spcaofcumber-
landco.bizland.com

North Dakota

The Natural Pet Center
1307 14th Ave. South
Fargo, ND 58503
701-239-0110

Pet Connection Humane
Society
730 Highway 1804 NE
Bismarck, ND 58503
701-222-2719
www.petcon.org

Ohio

Geauga Humane Society
Cleveland
Capital Area Humane
Society (Central Ohio)
3015 Scioto-Darby
Executive Ct.
Hillard, OH 43026
614-777-PETS
www.cahs-pets.org

Humane Society of
Allen County
3606 Elida Rd.
Lima, OH 45807
419-991-1775
www.hsoac.org

Oklahoma

Humane Society of
Stillwater
1710 South Main St.
Stillwater, OK 74074
405-377-1701
www.hspets.org

Pets and People Humane
Society
701 Inla Ave.
Yukon, OK 73085
405-350-PETS
www.petsandpeople.com

Oregon

Humane Society of
Central Oregon
61170 S.E. 27th St.
Bend, OR 97702
541-382-3537
www.hsco.org

Oregon Humane Society
1067 N.E.
Columbia Blvd.
Portland, OR 97211
503-282-7722
www.oregonhumane.org

Pennsylvania

Pennsylvania SPCA
350 E. Erie Ave.
Philadelphia, PA 19134
www.pspca.org

Animal Friends
2643 Penn Ave.
Pittsburgh, PA 15222
412-566-2100
www.animal-friends.org

Morris Animal Refuge
1242 Lombard St.
Philadelphia, PA 19147
215-735-3256
215-735-9570
www.morrisanimalrefuge.
org

Puerto Rico

Fundación Save a Sato
Villas de Cappara,
D-2 Calle C
Guaynabo, Puerto Rico
00966
www.saveasato.org

Rhode Island

Providence Animal
Rescue League
34 Elbow St.
Providence, RI 02903
401-421-1399
www.parl.org

Animal Rescue League of
Southern Rhode Island
P.O. Box 458
Wakefield, RI 02880-0458
www.southkingstown.com
/arl/

South Carolina

John Ancrum SPCA
3861 Leeds Ave.
Charleston, SC 29405
843-747-4849
www.jaspca.com

Oconee County Humane
Society
321 Camp Rd.
Walhalla, SC 29691-4811
864-638-8798
www.oconeehumane.org

South Dakota

Aberdeen Area Humane
Society
P.O. Box 1013
Aberdeen, SD
57402-1013
605-266-1200
www.anewleashonlife.net

Sioux Falls Area Humane
Society
3720 East Benson Rd.
Sioux Falls, SD 57104
605-338-4441
www.sfhumanesociety.com

Tennessee

The Humane Society of
the Tennessee Valley,
South Knoxville
Adoption Center
P.O. Box 9479
Knoxville, TN 37940
865-573-9675
www.humanesociety
tennessee.com

Texas

SPCA of Texas
362 S. Industrial Blvd.
Dallas, TX 75207
214-651-9611
1-888-ANIMALS
www.spca.org

Dog and Kitty
City/Humane Society
of Dallas
2719 Manor Way, Dallas,
TX 75235
214 350-7387
www.dognkittycity.com

Austin Humane Society
124 W. Anderson Ln.
Austin, TX 78752
512-837-7985
www.austinspca.com

Houston SPCA
900 Portway Dr.
Houston, TX 77024
713-869-SPCA (7722)
www.spcahouston.org

Martin Spay/
Neuter Clinic
362 S. Industrial Blvd.
Dallas, TX 75207

Utah

Best Friends Animal
Society
5001 Angel Canyon Rd.
Kanab, UT 84741-5000
435-644-2001
www.bestfriends.org

Community Animal
Welfare Society (CAWS)
P.O. Box 17825
Salt Lake City, UT 84117
801-328-4731
www.caws.org

Humane Society of Utah
P.O. Box 573659
Murray, UT 84157-3659
801-261-2919
www.utahhumane.org

Vermont

Addison County Humane
Society
236 Boardman St.
Middlebury, VT 05753
802-388-1100
www.addisonhumane.org

Frontier Animal Society
of Vermont
4473 Barton Orleans Rd.
Orleans, VT 05860
802-754-2228
www.frontieranimal
society.com

Virginia

Richmond SPCA
2519 Hermitage Rd.
Richmond, VA 23220
804-643-6785
www.richmondspca.org

Virginia Beach SPCA
3040 Holland Rd.
Virginia Beach, VA 23453
757-427-0070
www.vbspca.com

Washington

The Humane Society for
Seattle/King County
13212 S.E. Eastgate Way
Bellevue, WA 98005
425-641-0800
www.seattlehumane.org

Seattle Animal Shelter
2061 15th Ave. West
Seattle, WA 98119
206-386-PETS
www.ci.seattle.wa.us/
animalshelter

Humane Society for
Southwest Washington
2121 St. Francis Lane
Vancouver, WA 98660
360-693-4746
southwesthumane.org

Washington, D.C.

Washington Animal
Rescue League
71 Oglethorpe St., N.W.
Washington, DC 20011
202-726-2556
www.warl.org

Washington Humane Society
1201 New York Ave., N.E.
Washington, DC 20002
202-576-6664
or
7319 Georgia Ave., N.W.
Washington, DC 20012
202-Be Humane
www.washhumane.org

West Virginia

Berkeley County Humane Society
554 Charles Town Rd.
Martinsburg, WV 25401
304-267-8389
berkeley.wvhumane.com

Kanawha/Charleston Humane Association
1248 Greenbrier St.
Charleston, WV 25311
304-342-1576
www.wvanimalshelter.com

Wisconsin

Chippewa County Humane Association
10503 CTH S South
Chippewa Falls, WI 54729
715-382-4832
www.chippewahumane.com

Forest County Humane Society
701 Industrial Pky.
Crandon, WI 54520
715-478-2098
www.petfinder.org/shelters/WI62.html

Wyoming

Lander Pet Connections, Inc.
385 Del St.
Lander, WY 82520
www.webpan.com/pet connection

Wendy Diamond is the founder and the editorial director of *Animal Fair* (fairness to animals), a lifestyle magazine for pet owners. Her other accomplishments include two best-selling cookbooks, *A Musical Feast* and *An All-Star Feast*, featuring recipes donated by celebrities and athletes, which benefited charities. She is a leading authority on animal lifestyles, and in 2002, she starred in the critically acclaimed TV show *Single in the City*, where she and Lucky went off in search of Mr. Right Breed.

Wendy was born in Chagrin Falls, Ohio, and currently lives in New York with Pasha, her Russian blue rescued cat, and Lucky, her six-pound Maltese. And she's still searching for that lucky Mr. Right. For more information, please visit www.animalfair.com.